52 *Bright Ideas to Bring More*

Humor, Hugs, *and* Hope *into* Your Life!

Dear Nicole —
Hugs to you!
Greg

Greg Risberg, MSW, CSP
Virginia McCullough

52 Bright Ideas to Bring Humor, Hugs, and Hope into Your Life!

ISBN-13: 978-1-934792-04-9
ISBN-10: 1-934792-04-7

Published by
    Book Marketing Solutions, LLC
    10300 E. Leelanau Court
    Traverse City, MI 49684
    info@BookMarketingSolutions.com
    www.BookMarketingSolutions.com

Written, designed, and
printed in the United States of America

This book is available at
www.ReadingUp.com

Dedication

Greg wishes to dedicate this book to his wife, Madeleine VanHecke, a constant source of humor, hugs, and hope, but most of all, much love and caring support, and to his favorite (and only) grandchild, Claudia Rufo, who's mere presence in this world has provided much humor, many hugs, and hope for the future of our world.

Greg would also like to thank all the people who enriched his life by telling him their personal stories.

Virginia wishes to dedicate this book to her two children, Laura McCullough-Delorme and Adam McCullough, the best "bright ideas" she's ever had and her greatest sources of humor, hugs, and hope.

Introduction

Welcome to our book of short essays, inspirational quotes, and a few enjoyable exercises! We were motivated to write this particular book because Greg's audiences wanted to take away more of his message after hearing him speak. Our goal was simple: We wanted to present some helpful—and hopeful—ideas, the equivalent of a single concept per week for one year. So, consider these entries food for thought, snippets that remind you about some of life's enduring truths.

We'd like to hear from you. (See the back page for information about reaching us.) Tell us about an incident in your life that lifted your spirits, brought you closer to another person, renewed your sense of hope, or perhaps just gave you a good laugh.

We hope you enjoy our book, and we look forward to hearing from you!

Greg Risberg, MSW, CSP
Virginia McCullough

sometimes I find it very helpful just to stand in a daze for a while.

By Mary Lawton. Used by permission.

1

Say Yes to Small Changes

Most of us live as if the quality of our days depends on having or doing the big things: landing our dream job, finding the perfect home, falling in love, raising healthy children, or finally taking off on our "fantasy" vacation or adventure. For sure, these things dominate our thoughts and absorb most of our time. But have you ever noticed that even those who seem to have all the "good things in life" don't necessarily seem content?

When it comes right down to it, doesn't the quality of our daily lives depend more on the small choices we make than on the momentous decisions? And, as we all know, it's easy to sink into a rut. We do the same things in the same way and wonder why we don't look forward to each new day as a fresh beginning. Many of us worry or complain about dozens of little annoyances or irritations, or we may "sleepwalk" through our days without stopping to enjoy them moment to moment. Good news—it doesn't have to be that way.

To recharge your life, and to fill it with more humor, happiness, and hope, we ask you to begin paying attention to the joy and beauty found in what you may think of as ordinary experiences. We hope you'll open your eyes and look closely at the details in your life, the little moments, items, passing observations, and pleasures you may believe you're too busy to notice. We ask that you expand the space in your heart to allow in greater pleasure and peace.

Improving your quality of life is a choice you make every day. Think of it like this: A new day is a chance to take a journey to a place filled with the comfortable and the familiar, but which always offers fresh realizations, opportunities to deepen your bond with others, and unexpected moments of joy.

We hope you will accept our invitation to cherish everyday experiences and say yes to the little pleasures life offers us each day—starting right now!

Just a small wake-up call is all that's often needed to remind us of how powerful our choices are and what a difference the small choices each day can make in the course and quality of our lives.
—Melody Beattie, Author and Lecturer

There is no such thing in anyone's life as an unimportant day.
—Alexander Woolcott, American Writer

2

Look for Beauty

—or—

There's "Gold" in Your Own Backyard

Beauty surrounds us—but to see it we must be willing to stay alert. Luckily, we don't need to leave home to steep ourselves in beauty. How long has it been since you've taken a close look at the pictures on your wall or the birds sitting in the bushes outside your house? Look for beauty in a nearby park, a neighbor's garden, or in your own backyard.

When was the last time you visited a museum in your own city or town? Most of us wait for relatives or friends to visit and then we're surprised by how much fun we have! Some people like the idea of a trip to a local attraction, but instead of making plans to go, they immediately think of all the drawbacks: it might rain; parking is a pain; and there's always the old standby, too much traffic. Don't wait for a special occasion to take advantage of "free beauty." Pretend you're a visitor in your own city and see it with fresh eyes. Just say yes and forget the drawbacks—beauty always inspires hope in our hearts.

> *The only difference between an extraordinary life and an ordinary one is the extraordinary pleasures you find in ordinary things.*
>
> —Veronique Vienne, Author

3

Celebrate!

—or—

Every Day's a Holiday

How long do your birthday celebrations last? For most of us a birthday lasts 24 hours. But there are 8,760 hours in a year, so one day is actually a very short celebration. Then too, some years you may find yourself preoccupied or tired when your birthday rolls around, so your celebration isn't memorable at all. It's time for a change. Try this idea: One year, I felt bad that I was out of town on my wife's (Madeleine) birthday. We agreed to celebrate when I returned from my trip four days later. But then I thought, "Why not celebrate her birthday for a whole week?"

Our weeklong celebration worked so well that we expanded the idea, and at our house birthday "parties" go on all month. What a hoot it's been! We've had so much fun we decided to extend our celebrations to include all sorts of events, so between birthdays and holidays we have both planned and impromptu parties and celebrations going on all the time. September is our anniversary month, November and December provide weeks of celebration opportunities, and January is my birthday month. February gives us Valentine's Day, and our granddaughter's birthday month is March. As we move through months, even the return of daylight savings gives us an excuse to make the day special. And we can't forget Mother's Day and Father's Day. Overall, we've managed to find excuses to celebrate all year long.

The more you praise and celebrate your life, the more there is in life to celebrate.

—Oprah Winfrey,
Talk Show Host and Philanthropist

. . .we all need the reassuring and healing messages that treasured rituals provide.

—Sara Ban Breathnach, Author

4

Play! It's Not Just For Kids,

—or—

How Often Do You Go Out and Play?

Dance, paint, sing, take a walk with a friend, play Scrabble or Scattergories, work in the garden, or bake a cake. Find activities you enjoy and do them regularly—find the time. Your wellbeing may depend on it. Many of us forget that laughter and play promote health and happiness. Play may be the work of childhood, but our need for fun never goes away. Play is as important at 30, or 55, or 85 as it was when we were painting with big brushes in kindergarten or playing softball in the park. Having fun leads to laughter, and laughter leads to hope and optimism.

Can you think of three activities that you do just for fun?

1. _____ .

2. _____ .

3. _____ .

When was the last time you did any of them? Has it been too long?

> *You can discover more about a person in an hour of play than in a year of conversation.*
>
> —Plato,
> Greek Philosopher

5

Nurture Your Friendships,

—or—

"I Wonder What Happened to ...?"

Samuel Butler said that friendship is like money: "easier made than kept." Do you have a friend you haven't talked with in months or even years? How long has it been since you expressed your love to an important person in your life? Does a problem linger in one of your friendships? Too often we let even cherished relationships drift along, even stagnate. But it doesn't take conflict to make our friendships wither away; lack of water and weeding will do the job too. There will never be a better time to bring loving concern to an important friendship.

So often we hear stories of regret when a friend dies. These stories usually start with "If only I'd . . . " or "Why didn't I call . . .." When our hearts are free of regret, we have more love and laughter to offer.

After September 11, I received calls from three friends I

hadn't heard from in over 20 years. (They found me through the White Pages on the Internet.) These calls represented bright spots in otherwise difficult days. The old friendships began anew, but how much better it would have been if we'd never drifted apart at all. It took a tragic event to prompt this renewal.

Who do you think about from time to time? Who do you wish you could see or talk to? Don't wait for a dramatic event or even a tragedy to reach out to an old friend.

Fill in the following blanks. I'd like to find out about/ contact:

1. _____.

2. _____.

3. _____.

4. _____.

5. _____.

The better part of one's life consists of one's friendships.
—Abraham Lincoln, U.S. President

I believe that friends are quiet angels who lift us to our feet when our wings have trouble remembering how to fly.

—Author Unknown

6

Look at All Those Empty Chairs,

—or—

Those Who Eat Together Have More Fun

Eating out is a true American pastime. Did you know that the average person eats at least one meal a day away from home? How many casual conversations with neighbors or acquaintances start with "Have you tried the new Italian place?" Restaurants rank high on our list of discussion topics. We may even offer tips about the best time to go to a particular place and happily share details about our favorite evening specials. But have you noticed how many couples go out for dinner and end up staring at their plates or glancing around at other diners? They may talk a little here and there, but the evening ends up being just another ho-hum night out.

We can do better, and I have an idea. What if your favorite restaurant set aside an evening or two each week and offered the option of being seated with another couple or two? They'd set up tables of four or six instead of leaving all those tables for four with two empty chairs. The restaurant would serve more people and their customers would have more fun. I've talked about my idea with a few friends and they think it's a great concept. Oh, I'm sure some will say they don't want to share a meal with strangers, but a stranger is someone whose name we don't know yet. After all, we routinely chat with strangers on airplanes and in grocery store lines.

So, we're putting a formal challenge out to restaurants and readers. Give this idea a try.* What have you got to lose? If you have fun with your "stranger" dining companions, you might plan to meet for dinner again. Before you know it, you'll have made some new friends. And soon, other restaurants will hear about the innovative idea . . . newspapers will write stories about it . . . dining clubs will spring up all over the country . . . well, you get the point.

> *We call it the "herd effect," but a better way to say it is that eating is meant to be social activity—we enjoy the smells and taste of food more when we sit down together and share our meals with others. The earliest human societies knew that, but I think we've forgotten it.*
> —Alan Hirsch, MD,
> Neurologist and Smell and Taste Researcher

*If you manage to eat with some strangers, let me know. I'd love to hear your story.

7

Reminder:
You Are Unique,

—or—

You Really Are One-of-a-Kind

No one is quite like you. It may sound like a cliché, but it's true. Your gifts to the world are original because you are a unique creation. This is one of life's most profound mysteries and we often act as if we don't quite believe it! But, consider that your mother had about 6,000 eggs and your father had six billion sperm (give or take). And then, in one flash, one of each met and produced you! Ta da!

As Bernie Seigel said, "Life is an opportunity to contribute love in your own way." Today, remind yourself that you have special talents, skills, abilities, and potential to offer the world. Think of three qualities you offer to others.

I am unique because:

1. I am_____.

2. I can_____.

3. I offer_____.

What are you proud of? What qualities have you developed and nurtured? Do you share your unique qualities, knowledge, and skills with others? Would you like to share more? Just off the top of your head, list three things about you that you can share with those around you:

1. _____.

2. _____.

3. _____.

> *Every person born into this world represents something new, something that never existed before, something original and unique.*
> —Martin Buber, Author and Theologian
>
> *If you have a talent, use it in every which way possible. Don't hoard it. Don't dole it out like a miser. Spend it lavishly like a millionaire intent on going broke.*
> —Brendan Francis, Irish Playwright

8

Clip Cartoons and Inspiring Stories,

—or—

Seek Humor and Ye Shall Find It

Did today's Peanuts or Calvin and Hobbes make you smile or laugh? Cut it out and post it where you can see it. Or, send it to a friend and pass on the gift of a good laugh.

Did a particular story in a magazine inspire you or make you laugh? Tape it to your bathroom mirror or use magnets to display it on your refrigerator. Surround yourself with uplifting stories and cartoons and share them with others. I carry a pocket notebook with me all the time and I jot down the amusing, uplifting, or touching stories I come across so I can share them with my audiences. I note license plates, too. My recent finds include: YRUHERE, LIV TDY, and CILUVU2. My own reads: HUGS2U, which is a great conversation opener.

The funniest resource I know of is Funny Times Magazine (www.funnytimes.com). Each month the staff chooses 100 humorous cartoons and stories and sends them to subscribers. I read the entire issue the day it arrives, and I always see something clever and funny to pass on to my friends, and often to my audiences, too.

So, make it a goal to find two or three cartoons or stories each week that make you laugh. At the end of the month, you'll have at least 10; by the end of the year, you'll have 120. If you enlist another person to clip cartoons and stories, you'll have a collection of almost 250 items guaranteed to make you laugh. Be a humor collector, but don't hoard what you find—humor is meant to be shared!

> *If I had no sense of humor, I would long ago have committed suicide.*
> —Mohandas K. Gandhi,
> Political Leader and Advocate of Nonviolence
>
> *The important things in life cannot be gotten in advance. They must be gathered fresh every day.*
> —George Regas, Author

9

Go All Out for Adventure,

—*or*—

One Person's Bungee Jumping is...

Have you ever felt like you're riding along in a rut in the road? Most of us have spent time in that joyless place where hope is a distant concept. Nowadays, we've replaced the word "rut" with the fancier term "comfort zone," but the meaning hasn't changed. When was the last time you tried something new or had a really fine adventure? You don't need to sign up for a bungee jump or go whitewater rafting to have an adventure. Explore a road you've never traveled before or start planning a trip you've been dreaming about for years. Take a class or join a group whose focus or activity you support.

A few years ago, I decided I'd like to try canoeing, but I didn't know much about it and didn't know anyone who did. Then I came across an article about canoeing, and on a whim I called up a person mentioned in the text. The more we talked, the more excited I became. I learned I could enjoy a canoe trip just 15 minutes from my home in the Chicago area. Rather than waiting for my next vacation, I could get started on my adventure right away. The door to a new experience opened so easily, Madeleine and I immediately began planning our first canoe trip.*

What adventures would you like to bring into your life in the next few months? Adventure starts in the imagination—what are you off doing in your daydreams? What do you wonder about? Take a minute and write down your thoughts. Commit yourself to an adventure—you can start making it happen today.

> *. . . if I was honest, I would admit that it [adventure] was largely curiosity, the urge to find the why, the what, and the how at first hand, without simply taking someone else's word for it . . . adventure and I are old buddies.*
> —Ann Davison, Author
> (and first woman to sail alone across the Atlantic Ocean)
>
> *Still around the corner there may wait, a new road or a secret gate.*
> —J.R.R. Tolkein, Author

* Update: We tried canoeing twice, and with each paddle we injured our marriage. We hated this new "hobby." Then, a very kind person suggested kayaking and claimed it had saved his relationship. Madeleine agreed to try it only if she wouldn't have to be in a boat with me! I accepted her terms and we went out once—we had a three-hour trip and just loved it. Needless to say, we'll have kayaking adventures again.

10

Milestones and Moments,

—or—

The Action Takes Place between the Goalposts

Virginia once attended a workshop in which the facilitator asked the participants to quickly recall a favorite memory associated with raising their children. Virginia immediately flashed back to the many early mornings she spent playing music and dancing with her preschoolers in the living room. This memory was like a snapshot, clear and sharp. She could see the colors in the room and hear the sounds of her children giggling as they bounced and twirled. If she could relive one thing that happened more three decades ago, it would be those precious carefree moments.

To contrast that experience, the workshop leader then asked the participants to talk about their children. Virginia, and everyone else in the group, thought about the milestones—the graduations, first apartments, careers and businesses, weddings, and so forth. As important as these events were, they weren't touched with the same sweetness as a single almost forgotten memory.

In our society, we tend to measure life in milestones. We check tasks off our lists and work (why not "play"?) to accomplish our goals. We're encouraged to start college funds before our babies can talk, and it's socially acceptable to describe our kids in terms of what they've accomplished. We often talk about ourselves that way, too, and our lives may sound a lot like our résumés. But where are the deeper pleasures, the lasting joy?

Let's remember that while we measure the milestones, we experience our lives in moments. Think about the most precious moments in your life. You may be surprised by how "ordinary" they are.

Some of my precious moments are:

1. _____.

2. _____.

3. _____.

4. _____.

5. _____.

> *How we spend our days is, of course, how we spend our lives.*
>
> —Annie Dillard, Author

We don't remember days,

we remember moments.

—Frederico Fellini, Film Director

"Speed Bump" copyright Dave Coverly. Distributed by
Creators Syndicate. Used by permission.

11

Laugh at Least 24* Times a Day

(*But don't laugh while sleeping— it could disturb others.)

Have you heard about the researchers who discovered that young children laugh 412 times a day (give or take) while adults laugh only 15 times (and that's counting chuckles)? So the logical question is: Where did those 397 laughs go? Apparently, for most adults, life is no laughing matter. And the news gets worse; we may need the laugh track on some sitcoms to alert us to the funny parts. Sadder still, we sometimes say that a funny movie or a story gives us "a good laugh," as if laughing itself is a noteworthy event. (Is there such thing as a "bad laugh"?)

Did you know that laughter is good for your health? It is impossible to laugh and worry simultaneously, as laughter expands your diaphragm, deepens your breathing, and delivers more oxygen to your blood. Some studies suggest that laughter boosts the immune system, increases chemicals that help the body fight pain, and helps us stay alert during stressful periods. If laughter is seen as "internal jogging" then you could soon qualify for a marathon. Short of that, laughter is the best and surest way to lift your spirits.

Humor Hints

1. Humor is best shared with others. (We are serious about this! Middle-aged, solo laughers are often given a wide berth.)

2. If no one is around, risk it anyway. As the old adage we just made up goes, "It is better to have laughed alone than never to have laughed at all."

3. Next time you're at a family gathering encourage everyone to share funny stories. Start by saying, "Do you remember when ...?"

4. Ask others to tell their funny stories. Do this in a group and watch the fun and laughter grow.

I did this at a restaurant recently, when I was having dinner with people who had all just met. At some point I suggested that we share stories about embarrassing moments. Well, the stories got funnier and funnier as we went along, and we laughted so hard the manager came to our table and asked us "to settle down." This made us laugh even more. Want to have some fun at your next gathering? Try this.

> *Laugh often, long and loud. Laugh until you gasp for breath.*
> —George Carlin, Author, Actor, and Comedian
>
> *If you're going to be able to look back on something and laugh, you might as well laugh about it now.*
> —Marie Osmond, Entertainer

*Laughter helps me both relax
and recharge my batteries.
How wonderful is that?*

—Greg Risberg, MSW

12

Let's Go to the Movies—Take 1

The Top Picks for Great *Laughs*

Do you know anyone who doesn't enjoy a good movie? We don't either. And there's nothing like a good comedy. Greg conducted his own survey of crowd-pleasers at a number of events. While the results aren't exactly scientific, we think you'll like the top picks. Of course, some movies fit into more than one category (appearing later in the book). Perhaps some of the best movies make us laugh, cry, and feel good, as well as inspire us. And give us an unforgettable old-fashioned love story, too. So, mix and match to create your own lists—we didn't number them because they're all winners.

Patch Adams

Blazing Saddles

Liar Liar

I (Heart) Huckabees

Lady Killers

Airplane

Young Frankenstein

Life of Brian

Meet the Parents

Meet the Fockers

Train, Planes, and Automobiles

The Gods Must be Crazy

The Brother from Another Planet

I Love You to Death

A Fish Called Wanda

My Big Fat Greek Wedding

Napoleon Dynomite

The Jerk

Hitch

As Good as It Gets

Tootsie

Dumb and Dumber

Bright Idea #12

Kingpin

Bruce Almighty

All of Me

Something About Mary

Mrs. Doubtfire

9 to 5

Caddyshack

Weekend at Bernie's

Monty Python's Holy Grail

A Christmas Story

The Breakfast Club

What are your favorites?

1. _____.

2. _____.

3. _____.

4. _____.

5. _____.

"Speed Bump" copyright Dave Coverly. Distributed by Creators Syndicate. Used by permission.

13

Take a Step on Your Spiritual Path,

—or—

What's This All about Anyway?

Your spiritual path may involve practicing a particular religion, studying with spiritual teachers, praying, meditating, or feeding your spirit in the natural world. These practices affirm your presence in the flow of life.

Perhaps you become caught up in the hectic rush of day-to-day activities and have forgotten the spiritual component of your life. Today, think about the vision or set of principles that guide you. Make time to sit quietly for a few minutes and think about the vastness of the universe and your part in it. Are you curious about other religions or spiritual practices? Why not visit a new place of worship just to see what it's all about? Or, how about attending a lecture series or taking a class that teaches the basics about many spiritual paths?

Nourish your spirit and find your peaceful center.

Let all the steps I take today be in the right direction.
—Clare Hanrahan, Author and Human Rights Activist

We don't know all the reasons that propel us on a spiritual journey, but somehow our life compels us to go. Something in us knows that we are not just here to toil at our work.

—Jack Kornfield, Author

14

Express Your Gratitude

—Put It in Writing!

It's been said that on the average day, most people have more negative thoughts than positive ones. However, thinking about what we do have in our lives is a sure way to reverse the percentage. A few years ago, Sarah Ban Breathnach introduced the idea of keeping a gratitude journal and suggested ending each day by listing five things you are grateful for. Oprah Winfrey took the idea and spread it to her audience of millions, and now the gratitude theme that runs through her daily show.

A gratitude journal is a wonderful idea and literally helps us count our blessings. How about making it even better by beginning each day with listing five or ten things you're thankful for. Surely most of us can think of ten things we are happy to have in our lives. Start now!

Things I'm grateful for:

1. _____ .

2. _____ .

3. _____ .

4. _____ .

5. _____ .

6. _____ .

7. _____ .

8. _____ .

9. _____ .

10. _____ .

I've found a foolproof method for being happier—I simply count my blessings as often as I do my troubles.
—Glen Von Eckert, Healthcare Executive

15

Stop Telling People You're "Fine"*

"Hi, how are you?"

"Fine, how are you?"

"Fine."

What just happened? Well, not much. My answer to this scenario gives new meaning to the word FINE:

> F = Frustrated
>
> I = Irritated
>
> N = Neurotic
>
> E = Exhausted

I think that is what "fine" really means. When people tell me they're fine, I usually say, "Oh, sorry to hear that! How can I help?"

Recently, someone offered another interpretation of FINE—"Feelings Inside Not Expressed!" In fact, we heard a woman say that when a friend claims to be fine, she starts to worry, because "decoded," that means her friend is lousy, but isn't ready to talk about it.

I propose a better way to communicate. Instead of telling each other we're fine—no matter what—let's grade our days:

» A so-so day is a C.

» A better than average day is a B or even a B+.

» A bad day is a D or even an F,

» But a really terrific day is an A or an A+.

My system opens communication. Virtually everyone knows what these letter grades mean, and most people ask for more information. If this system doesn't grab you, then try these: "So-so," "pretty good," "I've been better," "I've been worse," or, "It's another day above ground."** Try to be more honest. Some people will think you're crazy (don't some already think that?), a few won't care, and some may be curious and ask what's going on with you. And that's the point where a real conversation can begin.

*Most people don't care anyway!

**Greg heard this response from a funeral director. Immediately hug any person who says this.

Unbosom yourself, said Wimsey. Trouble shared is trouble halved.

—Dorothy Sayers, Author

"Speed Bump" copyright Dave Coverly. Distributed by
Creators Syndicate. Used by permission.

16

Speak Those Words of Love,

—or—

Why Hold Back What's In Your Heart?

Have you heard the story about the Swede who loved his wife so much he almost told her? Well, laugh if you want to (and you should!), but I'm Swedish and I didn't hear those words often in our house. It wasn't that we didn't love each other. We just didn't say it in words, although we did show it. How often have you told the people you love how much you care about them? What are you waiting for? What's holding you back?

We all know people who have rushed home to tell their dying parents that they love them. Sometimes they get there in time and sometimes they don't. But why take the chance? Live in such a way that those you love know how you feel.

Sometimes we hold back expressions of love because we are in conflict with the person or have some unresolved issues that still trouble us. But we don't have to work out every single issue with a person before we express our love. No relationship is ever perfect, so don't wait for some nebulous time in the future to reach out to your loved ones. Nothing will lift your spirits faster than telling others how much they mean to you.

During a talk I gave in Chicago, a man visiting from England was so moved by the idea of expressing love he left my talk and immediately went to the phone and called his wife back home. "Joyce, I love you," he said.

The silence on the other end of the line surprised him. He waited as long as he could, then finally he broke the silence. "Joyce, don't you want to say anything to me?"

"Yes," she said, "have you been drinking?"

Sure, some people aren't used to hearing these words from you, but say them anyway. It's better to express your love now, while they're still alive, don't you think?

Who do you love? How do you communicate your feelings? Do these people know how you feel about them? Perhaps many people in your life want to hear how much you love them. Make a list—you might be surprised how long it is.

1. _____.

2. _____.

3. _____.

4. _____.

5. _____.

> *. . . And don't stop here—keep going! Love is not . . . a noun. It is a verb.*
> —Hugh Downs, Broadcast Journalist
>
> *[Love is] . . . a little haven of refuge from the world.*
> —Bertrand Russel, Philosopher

*Happiness is when what you think,
and what you say, and
what your do are in harmony.*

—Mohandas K. Gandhi,
Political Leader and Advocate of Nonviolence

"FIRST, THE POOP WILL HIT THE FAN, THEN IT WILL TRAVEL DOWN THIS CHUTE TO YOUR DESK."

By Ted Goff. Used by permission.

17
Stay in the Moment,
—or—
What's Happening Right Now?

Joan Baez once said, "You don't get to choose how you're going to die. Or when. You can only decide how you're going to live. Now." On a day-to-day level, the past and future usually distract us and take us away from what is going on at this moment. But pleasure and joy are always experienced in the precious now. So when we stay in the moment, we enjoy the gift of our senses, and savor the sights, sounds, and scents around us. Living in the present leads to improved concentration, more effective communication, and reduced "mind chatter" that causes stress and tension. If you need a reminder about what it's like to stay in the present, spend time with kids and you'll remember what it means to live in the moment.

Certainly, we may need to address problems that carry over from the past, and most of us create goals and plan for the future.

We may even visualize our goals and use various methods to keep them fresh. However, staying in the present moment allows us to focus on what needs our attention right now. Think about the pleasure of living without chewing over yesterday's mistake or last year's might-have-been. And why waste time worrying about an unpleasant situation that may develop next month or next year?

It takes practice to live in the moment; it's a habit that can be developed. The first step is to pay attention to your thoughts. If you find yourself drifting into the past or living in fantasies about the future, gently pull your awareness to the present moment. Make this effort for week or a month and see if you find pleasure in the small things around you—the so-called "little things" you miss when you meander away from the now.

> *Yesterday is history, tomorrow is a mystery. But today is a gift—that's why we call it the present!*
> —Author unknown

18

Hum Along,

—*or*—

It Doesn't Matter
If You Can't Carry a Tune

You hear one of your favorite songs on the radio, or in the supermarket while you're dropping a grapefruit or a box of spaghetti into your shopping cart. What do you do? Notice it and smile to yourself? Nod along with the rhythm—and hope no one notices? Gather a crowd and break into song or ask another shopper to dance? (Well, probably not.) But why not be bold enough to hum along? Think of it as one of many LLPs (Life's Little Pleasures). Besides, the music is intended to create happier shoppers!

Alone in the car? Sing along—belt out that tune (filling in with la da and de dum when you forget the words). No one feels pessimistic while they're humming, whistling, or singing along to some old favorite. And if you're in your house or alone in your office, dance a little, too.

We have opportunities to enjoy little LLPs nearly every day. Here are a few that come to mind:

- the smell and feel of warm towels when you take them out of the dryer;

- sinking into a hot bath;

- finding a $10 bill in your coat pocket;

- the first taste of a chocolate chip cookie when it's almost too hot to eat;

- running into a friend in an unexpected place and heading to a coffee shop to talk;

- watching baby animals;

- finding a parking spot (without going around the block);

- stopping to watch migrating geese crossing the sky;

- getting out of bed early enough to catch the sunrise;

- watching the sunset until the sun completely disappears.

Catch yourself enjoying your own small pleasures.

You can't do much about the length of your life, but you can do a whole lot about its width and depth.

—Anonymous

We are much more than what we do . . . much more than what we accomplish . . . far more than what we possess.

—William Arthur Ward, Journalist

Those proud
of keeping
an orderly desk
never know
the thrill
of finding
something that
they thought
irretrievably lost.

—Helen Exley

19

Renew Your Commitments,

—or—

Decide What's Important

Hope is alive when we make a commitment to something, especially a relationship. Over a lifetime, most of us commit ourselves to any number of individuals, including parents, siblings, a spouse, children, and for many, long-term friendships. We may also commit ourselves to beliefs or causes. When we feel hopeless, it may be because we have lost touch with the people with whom we have a committed bond. Perhaps physical distance has kept us apart, or an emotional chasm has developed and we haven't repaired it. We may say that lack of time has made acting on our commitment to a belief or cause difficult, but perhaps we have forgotten that we are part of a world that needs our committed attention.

Think about your most important commitments. Reflect about the reasons you chose them. It's likely that you felt a significant jolt—even your body said, "I want to be a part of this!" What can you do today to renew or revitalize these commitments to a belief or a cause and to your relationships?

1. I will call _____.

2. I will offer to help out _____ with _____.

3. I will ask _____ to join me in _____.

These sound like simple ideas, but actions fuel hope and bring positive results almost all the time.

> *I suspect the happiest people you know are the ones who work at being kind, helpful and reliable—and happiness sneaks into their lives while they are busy doing those things. It is a by-product, never a primary goal.*
> —Harold Kushner, Rabbi and Author
>
> *To love what you do and feel that it matters—how could anything be more fun?*
> —Katherine Graham, Newspaper Publisher

20

What Are You Saving This For?

—or—

Let's Use the Good China

Do you own things that you don't use because it isn't a special day or because you haven't worn the old thing out? Are you storing something that seems almost too nice to use? Most of us have things like:

• Good china we use only for special occasions... Christmas ... Thanksgiving ... Passover ... maybe birthdays, even though we've been eating most holiday dinners away from home. We leave these beautiful dishes to gather dust—or maybe we keep them packed away in boxes in the basement because we don't have the right cabinet to display them.

• Gift soaps that smell so nice and look so pretty. But we better not put them out or someone might use them! We really should save them for another time.

- Scented candles we buy but don't light because they're special. We save them for some future occasion.

- New underwear we hide behind the old stuff that we keep wearing . . . and wearing.

- The chair we like so much that we'd rather people didn't sit in it because we don't want them to wear it out.

Second-hand stores are filled with "best" clothes the original owners didn't wear because they were saving the outfits for possible future events. It's a sad day when we finally must admit that the clothes no longer fit (and never will) or might be useful only for 1960s or 1970s nostalgia parties.

My mother had a couch she protected with plastic—even as a child I thought of it as reserved only for out-of-town guests! Too bad the material disintegrated under the plastic cover my mother used to "protect" it. Without question, she took care of things she considered her "best," but when I look back I also see that she didn't get much pleasure from these items because they were used so seldom. In fact, I don't remember her ever sitting on her own prized couch!

With the exception of some valuable antique items, most things we save are easily replaceable and we're denying ourselves simple pleasures if we store them away. (What pleasures could be simpler than using fancy soap and wearing soft, new underwear?) So let's declare today a special occasion and bring out the good china and light the scented candles. Shouldn't we enjoy the things we're fortunate enough to have?

Think about some of the things you're saving. Which of these things could you use—and appreciate—today or tomorrow? And when you come across something you're "saving," ask yourself what you're saving it for. Isn't it likely you'll enjoy it as much today as you will in that far off "someday"?

The perpetual saver always lives in poverty.
—Danish proverb

21
Acknowledge Your Fears,

—or—

Succeed … Foot by Foot

From poets and philosophers to activists and generals, numerous men and women have offered wisdom about fear and courage. They tell us that each time we act with courage we limit the hold each of our fears has on us. But let's remember that fear is useful; it is one of our precious instincts and alerts us to potential dangers. In his book The Gift of Fear, author Gavin De Becker reminds us that fear is a gift necessary to our survival. While we often want to overcome our fears, we need to acknowledge the value of fear itself.

At one of my talks, I met a man who mentioned his fear of driving through tunnels, which happens to be a fear of mine. When you have a significant fear, it's comforting to discuss it with someone who truly understands. We offered each other support and practical ideas about coping —there are more tunnels in this world than you'd think. He told me he manages tunnels by imagining he's going through them foot by foot. "For every foot I go forward," he said, "I'm one foot closer to the opening at the other end."

I took his advice literally and began to concentrate on his foot by foot approach whenever going through a tunnel was unavoidable. And it worked for me!

We can also use this man's advice metaphorically. When we face challenges and act, we are inching toward the end, whether that's the end of a tunnel, or our first public presentation, or whatever we see as a risk.

Pat yourself on the back for those times in your life when you overcame fear with courage, even if you were scared and felt isolated and alone. Many of our great heroes and heroines experienced great fear, but we remember them because they forged ahead anyway.

Courage gives us hope that wrongs can be righted and hardship overcome. Your small acts of courage inspire hope in the rest of us.

Fears I've had and overcome:

1. _____.

2. _____.

3. _____.

The Promised Land always lies on the other side of the wilderness.

—Havelock Ellis, Psychoanalyst

Heroism consists of hanging on one minute longer.

—Norwegian proverb

We should never let our fears hold us back from pursuing our hopes.

—John F. Kennedy, 35th U.S. President

22

Stay in Touch,

—or—

Why Is "No News Good News"?

What does the expression "no news is good news" really mean? To some of us, it means that if we don't hear from our parents, children, other relatives, or friends, then everything must be okay! In other words, we sometimes wait until something happens or we have some news—often bad news—before we call or write. No wonder so many people report feeling lonely much or even most of the time! Studies have shown that the greater our support network, the happier we are. Is that so surprising?

This week, call a friend or relative for no particular reason, not to announce news, good or bad, but just to say hello. Or drop notes to a few people who live far away. Let them know you're thinking about them. One of the greatest gifts of the answering machine is that we have the ability to let people know they're on our minds without having to dial and redial numerous times in an attempt to reach them. E-mail has the same advantage, and let's not forget about the old fashioned postcard. Take advantage of modern technology or stick with the old ways—but stay in touch! Let "no news" be the exception, not the normal state of things.

> *The most beautiful discovery true friends make is that they can grow separately without growing apart.*
> —Elizabeth Foley, Author

23

Something New to Look Forward to,

—or—

"I Can't Wait Until..."

Let's face it, much of life seems more or less routine. Most of us keep regular schedules and we fall into comfortable habits. That's fine, but we may forget to make time for things we'd really like to do, which may involve seeking fresh sites or new people to expand our horizons and give us something to look forward to.

Julia Cameron, the well-known writer and creativity expert, recommends a weekly outing she calls the "artist's date." She asks her readers to do something off the beaten path, such as visiting a specialty shop or an out-of-the-way museum. We think everyone could benefit by adapting Cameron's idea and scheduling an event or activity that typically isn't part of their routine. Spontaneity is great, but like the artist's date, if we don't schedule some time for ourselves, or for a special event with family or friends, other demands are likely to get in the way.

Would you especially look forward to a Wednesday night or a Saturday afternoon if you'd made plans to do something new? It could be as simple as having lunch in a restaurant you've been curious about, or it could be calling to reserve tickets for a play you've always wanted to see and now it's coming to your town.

If you've always wanted to do "something," whatever that something is, will you ever find a better time than now? Something to look forward to could be as simple as scheduling a coffee date with a friend you don't see very often but whose company always lifts your spirits. Or, it could be fulfilling a persistent longing.

Virginia spent years watching figure skating on television before she finally bought a ticket for a performance of Champions on Ice when their tour came to Green Bay. She asked a new friend to go with her and for weeks they both looked forward to the event—and they weren't disappointed.

As a professional speaker, the world of airports, rental cars, and navigating in strange cities and towns are part of my regular routine. So when I'm home, I look forward to having dinner with friends or an afternoon drive to the Swedish bakery in the neighborhood where I grew up.

We know that a trip out of town is something wonderful to look forward to, but we don't recommend spending 50 weeks eagerly awaiting your two-week vacation. Think about taking a break from your usual routine and brightening your day by having some fun by yourself or with family or friends. Is there a person you'd like to see? A museum or park you'd like to visit? A performance you will surely miss if you don't buy a ticket now?

Here are a few suggestions. This week I can:

1. Call _____ and make a lunch date.

2. Rearrange my schedule and take an afternoon to visit a specialty shop I've been curious about for years.

3. Clip the notice about a lecture series at the local library.

4. _____.

5. _____.

My favorite thing is to go where I've never been.
—Diane Arbus, Artist

There is one thing which gives radiance to everything—it's the idea of something around the corner.
—G.K. Chesteron, English Poet and Critic

"Speed Bump" copyright Dave Coverly. Distributed by
Creators Syndicate. Used by permission.

24

Put Aside Your Own Worries for a While

Feeling isolated or down in the dumps? Maybe you're discouraged about the "state of the world," or perhaps your concerns are closer to home. In either case, you can lift your spirits for a little while if you can forget about your own concerns and the seemingly hopeless problems of the whole planet. The easiest way to do so is to look around and then do a favor for a friend, or volunteer to help someone who needs assistance right now.

What "random acts of kindness" can you "commit" this week? How about driving your elderly neighbor to the grocery store or fixing a meal for an ill friend or neighbor? Perhaps you can join a group whose goals or mission you support. Joining with others to work toward a common goal or to meet a current need is a powerful act of hope.

Inspirations never go in for long engagements; they demand immediate marriage to action.
—Brendan Francis, Irish Playwright

In a gentle way, you can shake the world.
—Mohandas K. Gandhi,
Political Leader and Advocate of Nonviolence

25

Learn a Little of Your History,

—or—

Who Are All These People in the Photo Album?

How much do you know about your family history? Have you ever asked your parents to tell you stories about their parents and grandparents? Even though we call ourselves a nation of immigrants, many of us don't know why—or even when—our relatives came to the United States, or how they lived in their country of origin. Without that information, we may miss an essential part of the "we" to which we belong.

For 51 years, I believed I was the only child of Swedish immigrant parents who met and married in Chicago. With their families still back in Sweden, I didn't have grandparents or even cousins around me during my childhood. Eventually, some of my Swedish cousins found me. And while visiting Sweden a few years ago, I spent time with dozens of relatives I never knew I had. What a wonderful surprise!

During that visit, I learned I had a half-sister, who is 20 years older than I, and the mother of four children. I was in shock! I also found out she was the "secret reason" that led my father to leave Sweden in the late 1920s. This information changed my life forever and gave me perspective on family history I'd never even imagined existed.

Based on my experience, I encourage everyone to reacquaint themselves with their family history. Maybe you won't make such a dramatic discovery, but who knows what interesting tidbits you might uncover in your family's past!

It can be humbling to think about how many of our ancestors arrived in the U.S. with hearts filled with hope. For some, the hope may have barely edged out their fear of the unknown. When we worry about our personal future, as well as the future of the country and the world at large, let's remind ourselves that our ancestors probably sought—and found—strength in their bonds with each other as they lived through tumultuous times. We can do the same now.

At your next family gathering, bring out the old family albums and shoeboxes filled with photographs. See who can identify the individuals in the pictures and note their names on the back. Today's technology enables us to make copies of old pictures and preserve this small part of a family's history. You could make a CD of favorite family pictures and give them to your relatives as gifts—and you don't need to wait for a special occasion.

Don't wait too long to learn all you can about your relatives and family friends. When our parents and grandparents are gone, no one will be able to answer the question, "Who are all these people?"

> *[Family is]* . . . *the we of me.*
> —Carson McCullers, American Novelist

Home is the place where,
*   when you have to go there,*
*   they have to take you in.*

—Robert Frost, American Poet

26

Let's Go to the Movies—Take 2

The Top Picks of *Inspiring* Movies —Those That Make Us Feel Really Good

Some movies may inspire us to try harder or just be better, more compassionate people. Others give us a shot of hope for the future of everything and everyone on the planet. Many movies help us believe in each other and provide a special feeling—a lift for our spirit—that stays with us long after we've left the theater. We may even shed a few tears over them, too.

Here the top picks from Greg's informal surveys:

Dave

Chariots of Fire

Secret of Roan Innish

Whale Rider

What Dreams May Come

A Man for All Seasons

The Land Has Eyes

The Sound of Music

The Natural

Music of the Heart

Pretty Woman

Polar Express

Rocky

Sandlot

Mystic Pizza

Winged Migration

Forrest Gump

Grand Canyon

Father of the Bride (I and II)

It's a Wonderful Life

Brian's Song

Mr. Holland's Opus

Phenomenon

Field of Dreams *

Fried Green Tomatoes

Philadelphia

Shall We Dance?

Now it's your turn. List the movies that inspire you or make you feel great:

1. _____.

2. _____.

3. _____.

4. _____.

5. _____.

*Fifteen years after the movie was released, the actual "field of dreams" still exists in Dyersville, Iowa. Visitors continue to flock there in the spring and the fall to play on the field—and you can, too.

27

Express Appreciation for Another Person,

—or—

You Don't Have to Be on a First Name Basis to Say Thanks

Have you heard the story about the volunteer fire fighter who was busy doing his family's grocery shopping when he received a page and had to rush away to fight a fire? Leaving his shopping list and items in the cart, he hurried off. Some hours later, he came back and learned that a person who preferred to remain anonymous had paid for his groceries.

This unknown person performed a tangible act that showed appreciation for a member of the community who regularly served others. The fire fighter was deeply touched by the gesture. How would you feel if someone was kind enough to perform this same type of service for you?

Appreciation doesn't have to be dramatic. For example, most of us are more likely to complain about bad service than to offer compliments for great service or food. When waiters or waitresses approach my table and ask if everything, including the food, is okay, I'll often say, "No, it's not." They may look puzzled or even alarmed, but then I add, "It's not good, it's excellent!"

Why don't you make a point of commenting on the good or excellent service you receive in restaurants and stores? Why not let others in your community know that you appreciate their efforts? Who might you appreciate today? We've started a list that you can finish.

1. Your child's teacher.

2. The wait staff in your favorite restaurant.

3. A public employee who is doing a good job.

4. One of your colleagues.

5. A neighbor's garden.

6. _____.

7. _____.

8. _____.

P.S. Most people are longing to hear some good news, so don't be shy about sharing stories. I've seen simple handwritten notes of appreciation pinned on bulletin boards in public buildings, or restaurants, or hospitals all over the country. You could make someone's day.

> *Appreciation—gratitude—is the memory of the heart.*
> —Anonymous

Silent gratitude
isn't much use
to anyone.

—Gertrude Stein, Author

28

Turn Off the Distractions,

—or—

Try a "Quiet Evening at Home"

In our culture, the television is often the "guest of honor" in our kitchens and dining rooms. Maybe we should call it the guest of "dishonor" because we all know it interferes with meaningful communication, not to mention laughter and play! The quickest way to enjoy time with family and friends is to turn off the typical distractions.

We have much more fun when we listen to each other with both of our ears instead of one. Even when we're alone, the radio or television can keep us from staying in touch with ourselves. Many of us become so accustomed to background noise in our cars, our offices, and our homes that we have forgotten the beauty—and value—of silence.

So, join with others during the next "turn off the TV" week. Try driving to work with the radio off and see how you feel.

Many of us find that silence allows creative, new ideas to surface and almost everyone enjoys the sense of peace that comes from spending time alone or with others in a calm, distraction-free atmosphere.

Limit the distractions around you and see what happens!

Television news is like a lightening flash: it makes a loud noise, lights up everything around it, leaves everything else in darkness, and then is suddenly gone.
—Hodding Carter, Historian and Author

[Television] . . . a medium of entertainment which permits millions of people to listen to the same joke at the same time and yet remain lonesome.
—Thomas Stearns Eliot, Author

29

What Is Your Purpose?

(And we don't mean single-handedly saving the world.)

Do you know why you're here? For thousands of years, the mystics have told us that our sole reason for living is to learn to love. Others believe that we are here to give service to the world. Still others think that our purpose is to develop and use the gifts and talents we are born with.

Whatever you do—nurse, computer consultant, lawyer, flight attendant, or ticket-taker at the movies—take pride in being good at doing something others need and find useful. No matter how we look at it, fulfillment comes from believing that the way we live affects others and the world. As William James said, "I will act as though what I do makes a difference."

Imagine how much hope we'd find in the world if we all lived with purpose and commitment. Would Jonas Salk have committed himself to finding a way to eradicate polio if he hadn't started with hope? Would Rosa Parks have taken her historic stand during the early days of the civil rights movement without the hope that ultimately, justice would prevail? Our most beloved heroes and heroines always acted from hope and lived with a strong sense of purpose.

While we made need times of solitude to look within and figure out our purpose, many of us find it helpful to meet in groups to talk about our goals and what we really want to accomplish. Sometimes, the whole idea of purpose can seem so lofty and even overwhelming that we become confused and frustrated. But when we share the process with others, we gain perspective and humor—no one person can save the world, and your friends and colleagues will help you remember that.

I often ask my audiences why they believe they're here. Most respond with, "I don't know," but others say, "to care for others" or "to learn" or "to love." A few believe their purpose is to provide for their families, and that means making as much money as possible! Many people tell me they think they're here "to make a difference, somewhere, somehow."

I believe that we can all find a purpose for being here. Get in touch with what you sense is your higher calling. And take heart—Leo Rosten doesn't mention "being perfect" and never making mistakes. Notice what makes you feel good or excited, or what gives you the sense, "Yes, this is why I'm here."

Our favorite words about purpose come from the author Leo Rosten:

I cannot believe that the purpose of life is to be "happy."
I think the purpose of life is:

> » *to be useful*

> » *to be responsible*

> » *to be compassionate.*

It is, above all

> » *to matter*

> » *to count*

> » *to stand for something*

> » *to have made a difference that you lived at all.*

30

What Does Your Home Mean to You?

Can you guess who wrote the following words about his home?

[Our house] had a heart, and a soul, and eyes to see us with; and approvals, and solicitudes, and deep sympathies; it was of us, and we were in its confidence, and lived in its grace and the peace of its benediction . . . we could not enter it unmoved.

Home means different things to different people, but perhaps the most common notion is that ideally, our homes should be our havens. Whether you live alone or with others, how do you feel when you enter your house or apartment? Are the objects and furniture special to you? If you could change one thing about it, what would that be?

For many of us, our home is like a close friend who knows us well and allows us to be ourselves. And what is a haven if not a sanctuary, a place that offers great physical and emotional comfort?

The only problem with the "home as haven" concept is that, ironically, the more time we spend creating our private spaces, the less we seem to open our doors to welcome others inside. Perhaps we find the "entertainment" books and "gracious living" television shows so intimidating that we almost never invite people over for a simple potluck dinner or a casual evening of conversation. Let's forget elaborate menus and special themes and just invite our friends over to share some precious time together.

We were surprised to learn that one of America's greatest humorists, Mark Twain, wrote the words we quoted above. Who would have guessed?

Few things, including clothes, are more personal than your cherished ornaments. The pioneer women, who crossed a wild continent clutching their treasures to them, knew that a clock, a picture, a pair of candlesticks, meant home, even in the wilderness.

—From Good Housekeeping, 1952

. . . my gift to myself has been to make my home my sanctuary—a place that rises up to meet me every time I enter the front door.

—Oprah Winfrey,
Talk Show Host and Philanthropist

31

Affirm Another Person,

—or—

Just Say It!

When was the last time you told a friend, colleague, or loved one what you treasure about him or her? Sometimes fear holds us back, often because we don't want to embarrass others or ourselves. However, our world would be filled with more peace, joy, and hope if we made it a practice to affirm each other.

The next time you talk to your child, co-worker, spouse, or a special friend make it a point to say something affirming. Use the examples listed below to generate ideas that work for you.

1. I really enjoy/admire/respect the way you _____.

2. You're so good at _____.

3. When I'm with you I feel _____.

4. The world is a better place because of you!

My good friend Rita Emmett (a writer and professional speaker) does this all the time, and I used to feel embarrassed by her affirming words. Now I realize that Rita chooses to be an affirming person and she makes me feel wonderful. She's like the actor, Jason Robards, who remarked to a friend, "It would be a shame to feel so warmly toward you and not tell you!"

Don't hold back. Tell others how you feel and watch what happens next. (Some people may wonder what you're up to—or even what you want! But don't let that stop you. Affirming one another brings us closer.)

Not one of you truly believes, until you wish for others what you wish for yourself.
—An Islamic expression of peace

In everyone there is something precious, found in no one else; so honor each man for what is hidden within him.
—Hasidic saying

32

Affirm Yourself,

—or—

If I Don't Like Myself, Why Should Others?

Is it easier to affirm others than it is to affirm yourself? Probably so. Most of us were warned about bragging! We may have learned the lesson so well we rarely acknowledge our own gifts and strengths—and that's too bad

Make a list of things you do well or qualities you offer to our world. Fill in the blanks and don't hold back. We all have gifts to share.

1. I'm a really good _____.

2. I appreciate my _____.

3. I feel good about the way I _____.

4. I offer _____
to others.

Forget about bragging! As the saying goes, it isn't bragging if you're telling the truth. You're acknowledging skills and qualities that you may have worked hard to achieve, or you are showing appreciation for the gifts you have been given.

Start treating yourself as if you're the most important asset you'll ever have. After all, aren't you?

—Anonymous

Oh God, help me to believe the truth about myself, no matter how beautiful it might be.

—Anonymous

33

Discover Healthy Pleasures

(Yes, they do exist!)

In the last decade or two, many of us have become discouraged because we hear that so many things we once enjoyed are bad for us. The list seems endless—coffee, sugar, too much exercise, not enough exercise, too much work, not enough activity, and too much or too little time in the sun.

I often hear men and women in my audiences lament that "everything I like is either fattening or sinful in some way." On the other hand, we hear that we'll live longer if we eat lots of fruits and vegetables. Or maybe, it will just seem longer if we deprive ourselves of all the fun stuff.

Don't give up! Researchers David Sobel, MD, and Robert Ornstein, PhD, tell us that the pursuit of pleasure is essential for survival and health! If we didn't seek the pleasures of eating great food, enjoying sex, and seeking other sensory experiences, the human race would have died out long ago. These authors call this pursuit "the Pleasure Principle," and recommend that we sharpen our senses and rediscover enjoyment in everyday experiences and events. They suggest that we:

• Notice the aromas that surround us and enjoy the smells and tastes of delicious food and the fragrances of nature.

• Remember the importance of touch and realize that a caring touch is good for us.

• Pay attention to the familiar sights in our environment and literally bring more light into our lives—light is good for our health!

• Listen to the sounds around us, and also realize that music influences our heart rate, blood pressure, and levels of stress hormones released by our bodies.

And, no matter what, remember to laugh. I believe laughter and caring touch are the premiere healthy pleasures!

> . . . *the healthiest people seem to be pleasure-loving, pleasure-seeking, pleasure creating individuals . . . Good health is much closer to home (and more enjoyable) than we had imagined. It derives from pursuit of healthy pleasures.*
>
> —Robert Ornstein and David Sobel,
> Authors and Researchers
>
>
> *A good laugh and a long sleep are the best cures in the doctor's book.*
>
> —Irish proverb

"Speed Bump" copyright Dave Coverly. Distributed by Creators Syndicate. Used by permission.

34

Cultivate the "E" Response,

—or—

What's All the Excitement About?

Some people seem to be naturally enthusiastic about life. These are the folks who enjoy the weather even when everyone else is griping. They're easy to spot as they jump into new projects with energy and vitality. They greet each person with genuine love and concern.

Enthusiastic people do have their troubles and down days, too. But somehow, their spirit of hope prevails. Think about this: Can you be enthusiastic and hopeless at the same time? Those two concepts don't fit; they don't belong to the same puzzle. If enthusiasm seems like a distant friend, get back in touch with it. You'll see that your sense of hope returns the first second you feel the rush of enthusiasm flowing through you. It's true that some find enthusiastic folks are a bit odd, but so what?

What are you enthusiastic about today? If you can't think of anything immediately, then look for something. If you still can't find anything, fall back on this fact: On an average day in the U.S., about 6,200 people die, so if you're reading this, you're not one of them. You're alive—and that's something to be enthusiastic about!

Remember that enthusiasm isn't reserved for the major events in life. The small things count, too. Revive your E-response to life.

> *A champion runner doesn't even know he's in the race: He runs because he loves it.*
>
> —Anonymous
>
> *I have never started a day when I knew what challenges and joys it would bring. And that fact makes each day an exciting adventure.*
>
> —Greg Risberg, MSW

35

Pave the Way for Others,

—or—

We All Stand on Big Shoulders

We may not realize it, but we are not only role models for kids—we are role models for each other, too. And we are the beneficiaries of the hard work others have done to improve our world, literally standing on the shoulders of those who came before us. Of course, some of the most important pioneers are barely remembered, and many weren't appreciated in their own time. On the other hand, we've given some of them their own national holidays.

Let's be grateful for all the men and women whose struggles paved our way, and remember that we can choose to make our lives count, too. That's what the current mentoring movement is all about. Many of us think of our parents' shoulders and feel deep gratitude for their great efforts to give us all the advantages they could. Our grandparents may have played a big role as well.

If you can, ask your relatives to tell you stories about their early lives. Your interest will both affirm them and expand your love and gratitude for them.

Hopelessness can prevail when we forget we are part of history, that what we do matters. When we lack hope, it seems as if nothing counts. But hope thrives when we think of our lives as a continuation of what has come before, with—we trust—a few improvements along the way. Think about what you doing today that paves the way for others.

The piece on the following page is adapted from the original Prologue to Bertrand Russell's autobiography. Russell (1872-1970), a philosopher and mathematician, won the Nobel Prize for literature for his History of Western Philosophy.

Greg read these words decades ago and their message influenced the way he has tried to live. We now offer these thoughts to you.

What I Have Lived For

Three passions, simple but overwhelmingly strong, have governed my life: the longing for love, the search for knowledge, and great sadness at the suffering of mankind. These passions, like great winds, have taken me from one task to another, over a deep ocean of sadness, to the very edge of despair.

I have sought love, first, because it brings ecstasy—a pleasure so great that I would often have sacrificed all the rest of life for a few hours of this joy. I have sought it, next, because it relieves loneliness--that terrible loneliness that exists in absence of love.

With equal passion I have sought knowledge. I have wished to understand the hearts of men. I have wished to know why the stars shine. A little of this, but not much, I have achieved.

Love and knowledge, so far as they were possible, led upward toward the heavens. But always great sadness brought me back to earth. Sounds of cries of pain fill my heart. Children in famine, victims being tortured, helpless old people a heavy burden to their children, and the whole world of loneliness, poverty, and pain human life less than it should be. I want to lessen the suffering of mankind, but I cannot, and I too suffer.

This has been my life. I have found it worth living, and would gladly live it again if the chance were offered me.

—Bertrand Russell

It's only when we truly know and understand that we have a limited time on earth—and that we have no way of knowing when our time is up—that we begin to live each day to the fullest, as if it was the only one we had.
—Elisabeth Kubler-Ross, MD,
Advocate for the Dying

Pick battles big enough to matter, small enough to win.
—Jonathon Kozol,
Educator and Children's Advocate

36

Tell Me Your Story,

—or—

Move Over Studs Terkel!

What do we do when we want to become better acquainted with someone? We usually ask questions that can be answered with a story. How did you meet your husband? What prompted your move to Chicago? What was the best day of your London trip? What's your favorite movie? For many of us, one of life's great pleasures is becoming immersed in a story, whether it's on a screen or in a book, or best of all, coming from a person telling an intriguing tale.

In recent years, high schools and universities have started oral history projects, which involve interviewing older individuals in the community about their experiences and life lessons. This work was inspired by radio legend Studs Terkel, who has spent a lifetime collecting stories and sharing them with listeners and readers. Recent oral history initiatives represent an innovative method for recording the history of a community and capturing memories and impressions of everyday life.

Currently, we're seeing rapid growth in the personal history movement, which encourages us to, among other things, interview our parents and coax them to tell their stories. Some men and women turn these interviews into written family histories, not just a dry narrative of the facts, but a series of stories that describe the sights, sounds, and smells of the past. These family history projects provide words to go with the photos in the albums and the boxes of postcards and souvenirs from trips and special milestones. If we're lucky, our parents and grandparents may have left behind letters and diaries; however, recent generations are more likely to leave appointment books and home videos than personal letters or journals. So the time has never been better to tell our stories and pass them along to family and friends.

Tell me your story and you'll live in my heart forever.
—Indian proverb

What is a story? asked the child.

A story is like a star, answered the old woman. It is born in the past, illuminates the present, and will shine in the future.

—J.R. Carroll, Writer

37

Find Role Models for Hope

Your role models for hope might be famous and shared by many of us. Who would not consider Mother Teresa, or Mahatma Ghandi, or the Dalai Lama role models for hope? We can all share in their strength and the way they lived their hope-inspired lives.

But many of our role models for hope are probably closer to home. Think about your parents and grandparents. Some of us are related to people who left old lives behind, and with hope in their hearts, started over in a new country. Others among us come from people who, on the surface, had no reason for hope, but they carried on in spite of the odds against them.

Your role models for hope might include a baby who is learning to walk. The baby falls down again and again but gets up and tries once more. Perhaps you know people who have been told that their condition or illness is hopeless, but they beat the statistics and experience healing. I once chatted with a woman who had heard one of my talks. As we spoke about hope, she told me she'd been coping with cancer for 15 years. "Some days," she said, "all I have is hope." At that moment, she became one of my role models for hope.

Who are your role models for hope? Make a list of five individuals who inspire hope in you. Think about them when you're feeling discouraged and hopeless.

1. _____.

2. _____.

3. _____.

4. _____.

5. _____.

> *No one knows enough to be a pessimist.*
>
> —Wayne Dyer,
> PhD, Teacher, Author, and Speaker
>
> *Life is a promise; fulfill it.*
>
> —Mother Teresa,
> Missionary and Humanitarian

38

Let's Go to the Movies—Take 3

Movies that *Touch Our Hearts*

Movies often make us cry because we identify with universal stories of love and family, and sometimes loss. Many bring on tears because they deal with sadness or tragedy. Whatever the storyline, these touching movies are unforgettable.

Terms of Endearment

The Color Purple

Dead Poets Society

Boys Don't Cry

Million Dollar Baby

Field of Dreams

Rudy

Beaches

Scent of a Woman

Philadelphia

Pride of the Yankees

On Golden Pond

Steel Magnolias

Fried Green Tomatoes

What's Eating Gilbert Grape

Mr. Holland's Opus

Pearl Harbor

Bridges of Madison County

Love Story

Brian's Song

It's a Wonderful Life

Life Is Beautiful

The Notebook

Once Around

On the Waterfront

Stand by Me

Legends of the Fall

Father of the Bride I & II

Old Yeller

Rocket Gibraltar

Create your own list. You probably can think of a few that brought on some tears.

1. _____ .

2. _____ .

3. _____ .

4. _____ .

5. _____ .

"Speed Bump" copyright Dave Coverly. Distributed by Creators Syndicate. Used by permission.

39

Be Present with Others,

—or—

Where Did My Mind Go?

It's difficult to enjoy the company of a person who is physically present but mentally miles away. Even more troubling, this kind of distant listening is difficult to hide and the other person naturally feels slighted. You probably know the feeling—from both sides. The body is there but the mind is back in the office, making to-do lists, or worrying about something or someone. Yet our relationships are enriched when we "show up" for them.

If you find yourself distracted or drifting away from a conversation, ask yourself why it's difficult to pay attention. If you are unable to listen at that moment, can you ask that the conversation be postponed until you can give it your full attention? Are you willing to listen at a future time?

Perhaps you could say, "I'm exhausted right now, but I'd like to talk when I can give you my full attention. How about tomorrow morning?" If we clarify that we want to listen but are unable to at that moment, we send the message that we care.

The time we spend with others is precious, and one of the most important ways we have to affirm our relationships is by paying attention to what others need to talk about without letting our own concerns get in the way. Some of us have fallen into the habit of allowing our mind to drift away during conversations, and we may not even realize what we're doing. It may take practice to focus on the present, but our efforts will pay off in the long run. Nothing improves interaction with others more than caring attention and really being present for them.

> *We come back to live in the wonderful present, to plant our heart's garden with good seeds, and to make strong foundations of understanding and love.*
> —Thich Nhat Hahn,
> Buddhist Monk and Teacher
>
> *With thee conversing I forget all time.*
> —John Milton, Poet

40

Soaring with Music,

—or—

May I Have This Dance?

It's been said that we can't be depressed and sing at the same time—and it's true! But we can be moved by music and feel great joy or bittersweet nostalgia, and we can become exhilarated, too. Music we love often makes us tearful and a little sad, and most of us welcome the sense of being deeply touched.

We can use music to establish an atmosphere for creative work, to energize and entertain us on a long drive, or to uplift us and take us out of our own thoughts, at least for a while. Get tapes or CDs of songs you like and keep them handy so you can always change your mood.

I can bring a "D" grade day up to a solid "A" simply by singing along to "Celebration" or "We Are Family," or just about any of the old Beatles' songs. I used to have my favorites on records, and then tapes, and now CDs. With a little effort, you can put together your own favorites from all the old tapes you have around—your very own "Best of . . ." collection. And don't forget to get up and dance to your favorites. Can you dance and feel depressed at the same time? I don't think so!

Make a list of your favorite songs. We've started the list with a couple of Greg's favorites.

1. Disco Inferno

2. Celebration!

3. We are Family

4. Imagine

5. _____

6. _____

7. _____

8. _____

9. _____

10. _____

There's only two ways to sum up music: either it's good or bad. If it's good, you don't mess about it; you just enjoy it.
—Louis Armstrong, American Jazz Musician

41

When You're Feeling Down, Ask Yourself,

"What Am I Out of Sorts About?"

We've all experienced a vague sense of dissatisfaction or a temporary case of the blues. While these feelings usually pass, they are visitors that can bring valuable messages. Try to discover what the messengers are telling you. (And telling everyone you're "fine" makes it harder.) Just acknowledging your feelings can help you work out your difficulties and find solutions to life's ordinary problems.

A few years ago, things weren't going well for me, and Madeleine suggested we take a walk just to get out of the house. While we were walking in the neighborhood, she asked me a simple question: "What are you out of sorts about?" Out popped one possibility, then two, and three, and so on. Soon I discovered there were about 16 things bugging me and leaving me feeling out of sorts. These were small irritations and disappointments that had built up over a couple of weeks or so, and taken together they had me feeling down. Just listing them and acknowledging their presence in the light of day (or the light of the moon) immediately lifted my mood. The fact that a person who cared about me showed willingness to listen to my list helped enormously. I also found that most items on my list could be resolved or handled fairly easily. That's the value of giving voice to even the small concerns that occupy us.

Can you talk with your partner, or a friend who is willing to listen, about the small things that have you feeling out of sorts? What's on your list today? You should feel better by listing them.

1. _____ .

2. _____ .

3. _____ .

4. _____ .

5. _____ .

Big things? Small things? Issues you've been avoiding? Things to let go of? Something to act on? It's time to take the next step.

> *If you don't tell the truth about yourself, you cannot tell it about other people.*
>
> —Virginia Woolf, Author

42

Practice Kindness

If you knew you would die tomorrow, do you think you'd say, "I wasted too much time being kind—I sure wish I'd been more thoughtless and nasty"? Every person probably has a few regrets, but it's doubtful that being too kind would be one of them.

Some people naturally seem to be more kind and thoughtful than others—and they are generally people we admire. Contrary to popular belief, being kind does not mean being meek or a doormat. The late Arthur Ashe, a fierce tennis competitor and a dedicated human rights activist, was also said to be an especially kind person, even when he was under great pressure and his life was filled with personal sorrow. Eleanor Roosevelt, one of the most admired women of the twentieth century, is known as much for her kindness and unwavering hope as she is for her accomplishments on the national and international stage.

I carry around some Sugar Daddies, a kind of candy that's been around for a long time. When someone helps me out (usually a woman), or I see someone who's obviously having a bad day, I'll stop and ask, "Are you married?"

Naturally, the person is a bit surprised, but no matter what the answer is, I say, "Then you could use a Sugar Daddy," and I give her (or sometimes him) the little treat.

It seems that no one can resist a Sugar Daddy. Everyone smiles and laughs, and so do I. I guess this is my one small way to make the day just a bit more enjoyable for another person— and me, too. I recently heard about a man who likes to hand out Hershey's Hugs when he encountered someone he thought might need a hug.

Near the end of his life, philosopher Aldous Huxley was asked if he had any final thoughts he wanted to pass on to humankind. "All we need to do," he said, "is be a little kinder toward each other." Wow! After a lifetime spent studying the nature of human life and cultivating spiritual values, for Huxley, hope for humanity came down to kindness!

It is quite clear that everyone needs peace of mind. The question, then, is how to achieve it. Through anger we cannot; through kindness, through love, through compassion, we can achieve one individual's peace of mind.

—The Dali Lama, Tibetan Monk and Leader

Peace cannot be kept by force. It can only be achieved by understanding.

—Albert Einstein,
Physicist and Human Rights Advocate

"Speed Bump" copyright Dave Coverly. Distributed by
Creators Syndicate. Used by permission.

43

Get Off the Highway—Nature Is Waiting

Each time we drive to our summer home Madeleine and I drive past the exit for a state park, and every time we pass it I say, "Someday, I'd like to stop there." After hearing this so many times, Madeleine finally responded, "Since you mention that every time we pass it, why don't we just stop?" Good question. That day, we pulled off the highway and took a walk on a nature trail in the park, and I'm so glad we did. It's a lovely place, and we've made a point of stopping several times since.

Poets and artists have always reminded us of nature's power to renew and replenish our spirits. Our need for nature is obvious when we consider that wise city planners allocate land for parks and other "green space." The flower boxes on back porches or balconies of apartment buildings reinforce our need to make nature part of our everyday lives. Although it's fun and self-nurturing to leave home and walk through a park or stroll along the beach, we can't necessarily do that every day. But we can stop for a minute to watch squirrels scampering through the neighborhood or close our eyes and listen to the bird singing in our own backyard.

Did you know researchers have found that gazing at a waterfall can lift your mood, and that sitting quietly in front of an indoor aquarium can increase alpha waves in the brain? Alpha waves increase in a relaxed, meditative state, which in turn may reduce stress and lower your blood pressure.

Symbolically, spring may be the season of renewal and hope, but every day's sunrise tells us that we are a part of the ongoing life on the planet. When you can, get off the highway, so to speak, and enjoy the beauty your surroundings offer and increase your connection with the cycle of life.

To me, every hour of the light and dark is a miracle.
—Walt Whitman

44

Remember the "Hope" Map,

—or—

What Were These People Thinking?

Did you know that 49 of our 50 states* have a town called Hope? And not necessarily just plain "Hope either." Mt. Hope, New Hope, and South Hope all exist. Isn't that amazing? It certainly provides a glimpse of early settlers' optimism.

Although they don't appear in every state, we can also find towns like Freedom and Friendship, both in Maine, and Loyal and Luck, two towns in Wisconsin. And we can't forget Harmony, Rhode Island and Liberty, South Carolina. Should we be any less optimistic about our country's future than the individuals who gave their towns these names? After all, we don't see many towns named Loneliness or Hate.

When you travel to other states, take a good look at the map to see if you'll be passing through a town named Hope, or Harmony, or another one of the more cheerful concepts. See if you can find out how the place got its name. When I passed through Hope, Illinois, someone told me that the same person had founded towns named Faith and Charity. Unfortunately, Faith and Charity are gone, but Hope remains.

What gives you hope? For many, it's a new day. Make a list of some things that give you hope. We've already started with some of our favorites.

1. A new baby

2. The first spring flowers

3. A sunrise

4. _____.

5. _____.

6. _____.

> We must accept finite disappointment, but we must never lose infinite hope.
>
> —Martin Luther King, Jr.
> Minister and Civil Rights Leader

*Hawaii is the only state without a town named Hope.

Bright Idea #44

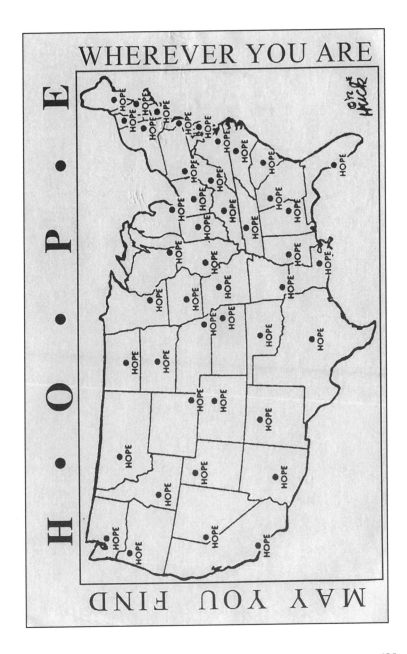

45

Nurture Your Faith, Not Your Fears

It's been said that fear is the absence of faith, and that fear is actually faith in the negative. In other words, if you believe in the things you fear will happen, then your fear is a form of faith. Individuals who possess strong faith don't deny that travail and even tragedy are part of life, but they focus on the messages intrinsic to the trials they experience. They have faith that what is happening to them has meaning, no matter how challenging the situation.

Those who live with faith are on a search for meaning and purpose, and hope is always a part of their journey. Faith also comes in many forms. For some, it's linked with a specific religion. For others, it's embedded in a deep sense that the universe and everything in it came into existence with intention.

People of faith tend to look at the big picture. How often do we focus on the small picture and find that our faith weakens? Have you thought about the bigger picture of your life lately? Take time to see yourself as part of the larger fabric. Our faith is often restored when we view ourselves as part of a greater plan.

Faith has nothing to do with odds. In fact, I once read a quip that faith means believing in something when commonsense would tell you not to.

Some recent studies show that people with a spiritual practice report feeling happier and seem to live longer, healthier lives.

—Greg Risberg, M.S.W.

46

Get and Give As Many Hugs as You Can!

When do you hug other people? When do they hug you? Do you hug others either when they're very sad or very happy? What about the rest of the time? Our low touch culture tends to reserve hugs for "special occasions." But a warm hug leaves us feeling great and brings us closer to one other.

One way to add hugs to our lives is to ask for them. Think about the people whom you would like to hug more often. Why do you or they hold back? Can you change that? If you ask for a hug and don't receive it, what's the worst thing that can happen? You'll feel rejected for a moment. Just remember that the person rejected your hug, not you. Sometimes I say, "Can you spare a hug?" Every now and then someone will say no, but most people respond with an enthusiastic "Yes!"

Most of the time, holding out our arms to others and offering a hug is a welcome gesture. Reaching out creates an atmosphere of caring trust. And we can all agree that caring and trust are desperately needed in our world.

The Hug Formula

The "Hug Formula" has circulated for many years now, but in case you haven't heard about it, here it is. You need:

- **4 hugs for a fair day**
- **8 hugs for a good day**
- **12 hugs for a great day**

How are you doing today? Are you close to a great day? Don't forget to ask for the hugs you need and want.

> . . . *the embrace—or hug—is the most dramatic and expressive touch we have. We embrace when we're laughing and playing, crying and grieving, greeting and parting, congratulating and supporting, and many other times, too.*
>
> —Greg Risberg, M.S.W.

47

Let's Go to the Movies—Take 4

The Top Picks of Good, *Romantic* Movies

We know that many a love story leaves us wiping tears from our eyes—at the very least. So, you may want to move some of the "good cry" or "feel good" movies into this category. Like we said, those responding to Greg's survey had a lot of crossover choices. See if you agree with these top picks.

You've Got Mail

Shall We Dance?

The American President

The Princess Bride

Four Weddings and a Funeral

Autumn in New York

Twelfth Night

L. A. Story

Guys and Dolls

Out of Africa

Dirty Dancing

Sleepless in Seattle

Always

A Walk to Remember

Ghost

Casablanca

Time to make your own list of romantic movies!

1. _____

2. _____

3. _____

4. _____

5. _____

48

The Golden Rule

By Any Other Name, It's Still the Same

 This is the sum of all true righteousness—treat others, as thou wouldst thyself be treated. Do nothing to thy neighbor, which hereafter thou wouldn't have thy neighbor do to thee.

—Hindu wisdom

 Do unto all men as you wish to have done unto you; and reject for others what you would reject for yourself.

—Islamic wisdom

 Hurt not others with that which pains yourself.

—Buddhist wisdom

 *Do unto others as you would have them do unto you.*

—Jesus of Nazareth

49

Focus on Possibilities,

—or—

Dream a Little Dream … (or a Big One)

Children are good role models when it comes to believing in possibilities. We rarely see a child who isn't curious and eager to explore the world and solve its puzzles. They usually impatiently look forward to the next activity or adventure because of the promise it holds. And they are willing to dream.

Until an adult manages to convince a child that a problem can't be solved, the child simply doesn't believe it. As adults, we often accept that the world is filled with myriad problems we can't do anything about. Sure, we can't individually take on every issue facing the whole planet, but we can strengthen our belief that no problem facing humankind is insurmountable.

Remember, there was a time when violence between nations was considered inevitable; it was the natural order of things and the only way to balance power. Today, many high schools and universities throughout the world teach courses in peacemaking and nonviolent conflict resolution. People who believed in possibilities made that happen.

> *The question should be, is it worth trying to do, not can it be done.*
> —Allard Lowenstein, Political Organizer

*The greater danger for most of us
is not that our aim is too high
and we miss it,
but that it is too low
and we reach it.*

—Michelangelo, Artist

50

Simplify, Simplify, Simplify

(Yes, this again!)

Everyone complains that modern life is too complex, too hectic, and just plain overwhelming. Sometimes the goal is merely to get through the day. Who has time to think about simplifying life? No wonder people abandon hope that things can get better. And it's difficult to find humor in life when we can barely catch our breath.

First, remember that you can stop spinning so fast, if only for half a day. The initial step in simplifying your life may be setting aside an afternoon to do nothing—no appointments, no chores, no phone calls.

The next step could be to evaluate how you're spending your time. You may find that you're spending time cleaning, storing, and fixing things that don't matter to you very much anyway. This is a common phenomenon in our affluent society. We also tend to fill our calendars with still more commitments.

For me, a step in simplifying my life came a few years ago when I heard about a terrible earthquake in India. Hundreds died and many thousands were left homeless. While on a trip to my bank, I asked the teller, who was from India, if any of her family had been affected. "Yes," she said, "and we're all so worried." When I told her I wished there was something I could do to help, she mentioned a specific need for men's clothing.

I went right home and started collecting shirts, pants, and shoes, and before long I had two cartons of good, usable clothing. The next day I took the clothing to the bank. When the teller saw items she got tears in her eyes, and we shared a warm hug. Other people in the bank noticed the boxes and asked what we were up to. The teller explained what had happened to her relatives as a result of the earthquake, and I later learned that within a couple of days she had eight boxes of clothing to ship to India. I was happy to have had the opportunity to help out, and the incident prompted me to finally clean out a closet. It took me about 30 minutes to significantly simplify my life.

For some, simplifying means having a garage sale to get rid of "stuff." For others, simplifying means learning to say "no" to new demands. Some make more drastic lifestyle changes in order to reduce both their expenses and consumption. The process of simplifying often means shifting the focus from quantity to quality.

What can you do to simplify your life? Why not begin the process today? Here are four ideas to get you started. You can fill in the rest.

1. Do any of the magazines that arrive in your mailbox feel more like a burden than a welcome surprise? Then next time you get a renewal notice, cancel it!

2. Any unused appliances lurking about in your cabinets or on your counters? Haul them off to Goodwill.

3. What about tapes or CDs that you haven't listened to in a year or more? Pass them on to a friend—let your old item be new to someone else.

4. Do your clothes multiply during the night? Maybe some item you rarely wear would look terrific on someone else.

> *Perhaps too much of everything is as bad as too little.*
> —Edna Ferber, American Writer

51

Love Really *Is* About Simple Things

Oprah Winfrey once had program on her television show that focused on the way families coped with loss. In one segment, Oprah talked to children who had lost their mother to cancer. That family was able to prepare for the loss, and they made a conscious decision to make the most of their time together, no matter how long it turned out to be. They did many things as a family during the mother's last months and years, including taking memorable family trips. But, when Oprah asked one of the children about her most cherished memory of her mother, the young girl said, without hesitation, that she'd always remember the time she and her mother ate Cheerios together in the kitchen in the middle of the night—just the two of them. Is it surprising that the girl's favorite memory triggered tears in Oprah and the audience?

Those who watch Oprah's television show regularly know

that she refers to this story again and again. She uses it when she and other guests discuss what parents and children, spouses, and friends really want from each other. Big events and lavish gifts are great, but we can never know what small event or a simple remark may be the most meaningful—and the most cherished.

Only the heart knows how to find what is precious.
—Fyodor Dostoyevsky

*There's more to life
    than increasing its speed.*

—Mohandas K. Ghandi, Political Leader
and Advocate of Nonviolence

52

No More Regrets

We hope you've enjoyed this journey and have brought more "humor, hugs, and hope" into your life. Perhaps no one better expresses our hopes and wishes for you—and for ourselves—than the incomparable Mark Twain. This is what he had to say about living fully.

Twenty years from now, you will be more disappointed by the things you didn't do than by the ones you did do.

So throw off the bowlines. Sail away from the safe harbor.

Catch the trade winds in your sails.

> *Explore.*
> *Dream.*
> *Discover.*

Good sailing to you!
Greg and Virginia

About the Authors

Greg Risberg is a warm, funny motivational speaker who has addressed over 500,000 people in 48 states, as well as Canada, Great Britain and Australia with his "humor with a message" programs. He helps people learn useful ideas for handling stress better, communicating better, and finding more balance in their lives. He does this with wit and humor that leave his audiences saying "your unique blend of humor, inspiration and message was perfect!"

Greg is an active member of the National Speakers Association, a group that awarded him their highest earned designation of "Certified Speaking Professional." He is one of only 500 people in the entire country to earn this certification. Greg has also received the Wordsmith award for speaking excellence from the Illinois chapter of NSA. He has a B.A. egree in psychology from

Roosevelt University and a Master's Degree in Social Work from the Jane Addams School of Social Work in Chicago. His work also appears in the anthology, *Humor Me*, a funny book about bringing more humor into our lives. For more information about Greg's work, visit his web site, www.gregrisberg.com

* * *

Virginia McCullough, a ghostwriter/editor for over thirty years, has written over 100 books and dozens of book proposals for doctors and other healthcare practitioners, professional speakers, and business owners. *The Oxygen Revolution* (Hatherleigh, 2007), coauthored with Paul Harch, MD., is the most recent of eleven coauthored books. She is a member of the National Speakers Association and the Authors Guild and has given numerous seminars on topics related to writing and publishing. A native of Chicago, Virginia currently lives in Green Bay, Wisconsin.

For more information about Virginia's writing and editorial services, visit her web site, www.virginiamccullough.com

Greg and Virginia coauthored a previous book, *Touch: A Personal Workbook*, and they've been friends for many years.

GREG RISBERG

*Greg's Most
Popular Programs:*

"You Make a Difference!"
This program helps people:

- Recognize and appreciate their contributions, talents, and abilities.
- Communicate more effectively.
- Realize that their efforts do, indeed, *make a difference*.

"Humor, Hugs, and Hope!"
*This upbeat program
helps people:*

- See more humor in their lives.
- Use humor as a stress reliever.
- Appreciate the importance of hugs.
- Feel more hopeful.

"How to Stay Energized in a Changing World."
This program teaches people:

- Proven techniques to reduce stress.
- Ways to relax under pressure.
- How to identify "good" versus "bad" stress.
- How to achieve more balance in their lives.

"That Goes Without Saying? - Improving Communication."
This program helps people:

- Be more effective communicators.
- Increase their sensitivity to others.
- Resolve conflicts more successfully.

We would like to hear from you!

Tell us about an incident in your life that lifted your spirits, brought you closer to another person, renewed your sense of hope, or perhaps just gave you a good laugh. We look forward to hearing from you!

Greg Risberg, MSW, CSP
Virginia McCullough

Email us: greg@gregrisberg.com

Write us: Greg Risberg, MSW, CSP
295 East Church Street
Elmhurst, IL 60126

How to Order

52 Bright Ideas to Bring More Humor, Hugs, and Hope into Your Life and other titles published by BMS are available online at:

www.ReadingUp.com

Quantity Discount

This title is available at a discount when ordered in quantity for your group or organization.

For bulk order information, please call: 630-833-5066 or E-mail: greg@gregrisberg.com